**MEDITATION FOR KIDS
AND BEGINNERS OF ALL AGES**

Meditation, My Friend

By Mitchell Hoffsteader
and Betsy Thomson

A Note to the Reader

This book was created to help inspire and teach
people of all ages to meditate.

Meditation, My Friend
Meditation for Kids and Beginners of all Ages
is copyrighted.

Mitchell Hoffsteader is an original Betsy Thomson creation.

Library of Congress Control Number: 2013910700

ISBN 978-0-615-32064-9

Betsy Thomson is the creator/writer, photographer, illustrator
and songwriter for this book. She is the voice of Mitchell Hoffsteader
and the audio portion of the book.
Kristine Tenner is the graphic designer and illustrator of this book.

FREE DOWNLOAD:
- Meditation discussion with Betsy and Mitchell
- Mitchell's songs: *Meditation Is Good For Me* and *Wish*
- Guided meditations

PLEASE VISIT:
www.meditationmyfriend.com
or email thomsonbetsy3@gmail.com

Special Thank You

Meditation, My Friend

is dedicated in loving memory
to
Mom Thomson and Dale Stearn.

And to everyone everywhere who helped
make this book possible.

Our sincerest and immeasurable thanks
for all your kindness, help, support,
and generosity.

We wish you much love, peace,
and laughter.

Mitchell
&
Betsy

Meditation, My Friend
By Mitchell Hoffsteader

Miss Millmont
by M.H.

Miss Millmont, my fourth-grade teacher, gave my class a homework assignment: We all had to write an essay on "What Makes Us Happy 😊 and Why." I can tell you what DOESN'T make me happy ⊗ writing essays! 🙁

I got on it right away the night before it was due. I wrote about how I learned to meditate and how doing meditation has helped me become a happier fellow.

Miss Millmont said that my essay was "A" worthy. But, she said it wasn't necessary for me to write a nine-page essay that included drawings and flow charts. She said I might as well have written a book!

Thanks to unsuspecting Miss Sarcast-o-Mont's twisted inspiration, I decided to write a real book! My BFF, Betsy, helped me out a lot. (You'll be learning more about her later.)

Now all you earthlings can read MEDITATION, MY FRIEND, the book that morphed out of my power essay. Hope you like it, AND I hope you meditate!

Your friend, Mitchell Hoffsteader

TABLE OF CONTENTS

Extra Hoffsteader Bonuses!

Chapter 1

Ahhh, I Have
Restless Brain Syndrome!

This is the true story of how I discovered MEDITATION.
AND how meditation became my friend!

Thank goodness!
M.H.

My story starts...

Please take care of him — we can't! His name is Mitchell Hoffsteader. He likes buttered noodles and being tickled behind the ears.

I was orphaned as a little fellow. First of all, I don't know who my parents were or where they went. It stinks! All I remember is that on one chilly autumn morning, someone I didn't recognize, a mystery person, left me on a doorstep in a mackintosh apple basket... *ALONE!*

Whoever left me on the stoop didn't even leave me with a juice box in case I got thirsty! The fiend. All they left was a note. I was crying because I was confused, scared, and mad. It was official. That day I felt so unloved and alone. I didn't feel like I was valuable to anyone anymore.

Why would someone abandon me? Surely you must be wondering this too. I just figured they didn't want me around because something was really wrong with me. Deep down I believed I was broken somehow like a factory reject toy. It made sense. Nobody likes broken toys, so I guess nobody liked me.

At least I was not on the doorstep too long.
Betsy found me the very same day I was dumped off.

It turns out I was left on Betsy's front doorstep. She must have felt real sorry for me because she adopted me right then and there.

Betsy is okay, I guess. She's sort of pretty. She'd be real pretty if she wore a little makeup or something. She could look like a movie star!

One good thing about Betsy is that she makes me things. Once she made me a papier-mâché astronaut's helmet. I wear it every time I travel to outer space.

I don't tell everybody this, but Betsy's hooked on reading her horoscope in the newspaper every day. Every time she reads it I hear her say, and I quote, "Oh, come on, who are they kidding, that's not even close," or "Oh, how amazing, it's like they know me." She's got me reading it now. I start by closing my eyes and pointing. Whatever horoscope my finger lands on in the paper is mine for the day. So far I've covered the entire zodiac the Hoffsteader way! Truth is, I really don't know when my birthday is because I don't know when I was born. I celebrate my birthday every year on Betsy's so I can have one too.

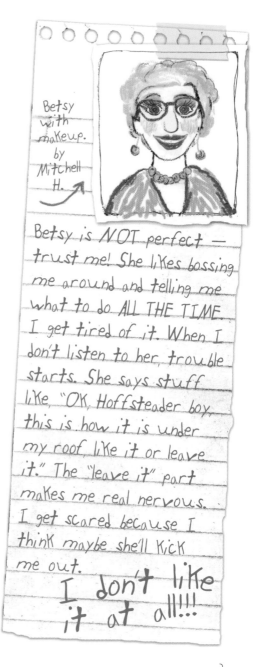

Betsy with makeup. by Mitchell H.

Betsy is NOT perfect — trust me! She likes bossing me around and telling me what to do ALL THE TIME. I get tired of it. When I don't listen to her, trouble starts. She says stuff like, "OK, Hoffsteader boy, this is how it is under my roof, like it or leave it." The "leave it" part makes me real nervous. I get scared because I think maybe she'll kick me out. I don't like it at all!!!!

Now you can see I'm dapper and surely effervescent.

Betsy and I butt heads a lot because nobody is going to tell *ME* what to do! Usually I can get her to buckle and give in to me with a lot of pleading and flattery.

Sometimes when I'm bored, I follow her around the house. I think it bugs her, though. When I do, she says, "Come on Mitch, you know I love ya, but go find something to do." I really wonder if she does love me. She doesn't seem to want me around a lot. Betsy's boring anyway.

I ask you, who says, "I LOVE YA," and then just walks away? I mean, really, it doesn't seem right to me. It reminds me of when the mystery person left me on the doorstep. They dropped me off, turned, and just walked away.

Luckily, as I got older I started to develop superpowers. Stuff like superhuman strength, X-ray vision, and the ability to make myself invisible. My secret superpowers were a lot more fun than boring Betsy's ignoring me.

But all my secret powers didn't matter. You know why? Because I was height challenged. I was SHORT! I NEVER seemed to GROW!

I ate whatever I could, and drank magic potions to help me grow. Nothing helped. Not even my superpowers.

Barbell Mitch

by Mitchell H.

Hoffsteader DNA

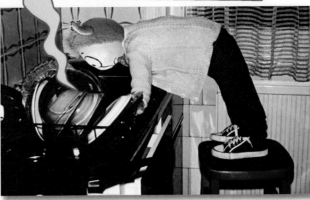

Obviously I was destined to be a scrawny little *FOUNDLING!* All of this affected my confidence and self-esteem in a big way. You know — how I believed I was an unlovable little shrimp.

I was different from the other kids and it really bothered me. I was convinced I'd never fit in because I was different. Who would want me around or would want to play with me? Sure, I had a few peeps Betsy would let me text from time to time. Thing was, they never ever wanted to get together and play with me. That made me feel really sad and lonely.

I was *PERSNICKETY* and a pro at acting out. That's what Betsy said.

Once I squeezed all of Betsy's radiant smile 3-D whitening toothpaste down the kitchen sink because I was mad at her for losing some of my Legos. She mysteriously lost them when she was straightening up my room AGAIN! My room was so clean I got sick.

Too much pressure was on me!

Turn off the TV!

Do your homework!

Pick up your Legos!

Eat your vegetables!

Now that I think of it, everyone everywhere was always telling me what to do. Do this, do that, blah, blah, blah. I just wanted to lie around and eat the junk food I snuck into the house. I always had to hide it from Betsy so she wouldn't take it away from me. Betsy doesn't let me do anything!

According to Betsy my taste buds are all dead. Why? Because of eating too much food that looks like orange styrofoam packing peanuts. *FACT:* A lot of the time I didn't do my homework because I couldn't concentrate. Too many squiggly thoughts were bouncing around in my head. *FACT:* I didn't care about homework anyway! Homework stinks!

I was a worrier too. I worried about monsters in the dark and under my bed. Who was going to help the innocent polar bears in the arctic circle? What will they do if all the ice melts? How will they survive? I even worried about being a worrier!

Some days it seemed I had no time for myself. I felt trapped. That was because of Betzilla's 👣 demands on me, way too much homework, and getting bored a lot. Even lady luck did not smile on me. Every Saturday I made sure to wear my lucky dinosaur underwear. That was when Betsy dragged me along shopping. My lucky underwear used to work like a dream. Whatever I asked Betsy to buy me, she did. One day I asked Betsy to buy me a boomerang. She refused. That's the day my lucky underpants stopped working. It was like all my luck ran out.

I had no time for galactic space travel or inventions in my secret lab. Worst of all, I neglected the ants in my free-range ant farm. I figured they could take care of themselves, and besides, ants are boring. They don't play with you. I built my ant farm on the living-room floor with fences made out of toothpicks. *FACT: Ants have no sense of direction or boundaries. FACT: Ants do not grow things on their farms.* All my pet ants left the farm in search of a better life. This got Betzilla going for sure! Was she mad! Ants in the cereal, under the couch, and even in Betzilla's bed.

If you ask me, my nerves were shot, because I got cranky and bit my fingernails. Even though I had a home and Betsy was sort of nice, I really didn't have friends, which made me sad. I wanted friends too. My only real friend lived in a tree so it was hard for us to hang out. He's a squirrel.

👣 = Betzilla...who Betsy turns into when she tries to catch me... distant relative of the late great Godzilla. Go to page 32 to see a picture I drew of her.

One day in school *I GOT IN BIG TROUBLE* because of my temper. It happened at lunch time. Sixth-grade bully and giant, Walter J. Patuziak, called me a "cootie-infested polecat" after shoving me out of the lunch line. I'd had it! Patuziak the skunk was going down!

When Walter's back was turned I tried kicking him as hard as I could. My aim was off. Instead, I slipped and fell right on my butt. Walter was laughing so hard he had boogers coming out of his nose.

Then all the other kids started laughing at me. They told on me and Walter. I was so mad. We both got in trouble. Walter got detention for a whole month because of bullying me. I think that scared him because he started crying. Principal Hooper locked me up in his dungeon. He kept shaking his head, saying, "What is wrong with you, acting like that, Mitchell?"

Then I started to cry. I had to sit there until Betsy came and got me.

Betzilla
strikes again!

Betzilla showed up instead!

Was she mad and embarrassed by what I did! Betzilla marched me right out of school and took me home. On the way home, she tried to lecture me about my bad behavior. I used my secret selective hearing to tune her out.

She threatened to send me to a "get the angries out" circle of care group for kids if I did not straighten up. I got really mad at Betsy because she never ever listened to my side of the story! She even knew Walter Patuziak was a bad egg.

I gave her the silent treatment until I went to bed. Deep down I feared I was turning into some kind of uncontrollable monster because of how I acted. I cried myself to sleep that night.

I wondered what was wrong with me. Nobody else seemed to act or feel the way I did. Sometimes, so I didn't have to think about certain things or how I felt, I'd turn into Captain Space Out. Then I could time travel to my Hoffsteader space-out zones. They were mysteriously located in the past and future, and only I could go there. I felt better there. Problem was, once I landed in a space-out zone it was hard for me to pay attention to what I was doing.

I didn't do too well in school either. I didn't care anyway. I got frustrated because it was hard for me to concentrate and pay attention. That made it hard for me to read and spell. I didn't tell anybody, even Betsy, because I just thought I was dumb.

I even stopped wearing my safety helmet when I rode my turbo-trike. Helmets were for sissies! I became a show-off too, just so people would notice me. A lot of times I was in a hurry and for no real reason.

My sissy helmet!

Hoffsteader worry #11

Would planet Earth be turned into an uninhabitable stink ball, thanks to uncaring Homo sapiens?

My friend planet Earth
by Mitchell H.

Sometimes I had a hard time sleeping at night because I could not stop thinking and worrying. Thoughts jumped around in my head all the time. No matter how hard I tried, I could not stop my thoughts. I had sad thoughts, happy thoughts, scary thoughts, mad thoughts, funny thoughts, all kinds of thoughts.

No matter what, my Hoffsteader head Kept racing with thoughts and worrying!

I stood on my head and there were thoughts! I covered myself with blankets; there were more thoughts!

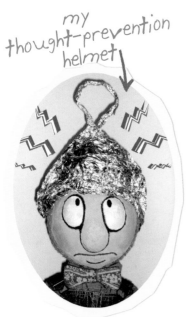

my thought-prevention helmet

I jumped up and down trying to stop my thoughts. I even made a state-of-the-art thought-prevention helmet but it definitely didn't help get rid of my thoughts. Especially my pesty monster thoughts. They scared me sometimes because they would sneak up on me from out of nowhere. *My worst monster thought was, "Nobody loves me."*

He was the meanest because he always made me feel bad about myself. He would scare away my buddy thoughts too, like, "I am lovable and I am smart." My buddy thoughts were always on my side! Sometimes when my buddy thoughts got scared away, it seemed like forever until they came back again to make me feel better.

One day it became clear to me. It was so obvious. *All my bazillion thoughts were causing me to have a severe case of Restless Brain Syndrome!*

I knew all about syndromes from watching TV commercials. According to the commercials there was hope for anyone with those syndromes. They were curable with "secret pharmacy potions" that caused screwy side effects. Side effects like googly eyes, webbed feet, an inability to operate kitchen appliances, mange, and worst of all, foaming at the mouth. That scared me. I couldn't go to school with a foamy mouth. I felt awful. This went way beyond a ten on my scale of doom, zero being no doom at all. Ten was the worst of the worst, *EEEETERNALLLL* doom. How could I cure it? Oh, what was I to do? I asked Betsy if she knew a cure for Restless Brain Syndrome. "Restless *WHAT Syndrome*?"

"*BRAIN Syndrome*," I shouted. Betsy assured me she did not know of anyone who had Restless Brain Syndrome. She said she never heard of it. She told me to take a chill pill and just relax. Relax?! Ah, what did she know?! I knew I had it and I had it bad!

Chapter 2
Oh No! It's Tenzin!

Once I realized I was doomed because of having Restless Brain Syndrome, I decided to skip school and run away.

I felt so bad. What was the point of even going to school? Everyone and everything was against me. Nobody cared about me.

If Betzilla ever found out I was playing hooky, I'd be busted for sure. She'd freak out and send me straight to my room, the tyrant! You know what? I didn't care. I was a rebel and no one was going to tell me what to do! I felt like running away, so I did. I snuck off to the park in my neighborhood. I went to my favorite park bench by the duck pond to sit.

Sneaking off was easy. I had to wait until Betsy was busy yakking on the phone. That didn't take long. She never even noticed me leaving. I backwards walked down the hallway to the front door. Then I backed out of the front door. Backwards walking was foolproof. If Betsy had caught me leaving she would have thought I was coming in instead of going out. It's an old spy trick.

I felt so sad and gloomy sitting on the bench alone, I started to cry. Things got worse, too. I realized I forgot to bring peanuts with me. I was so busy trying to sneak out of the house I forgot peanuts. Ah nuts, I wasn't

thinking clear again. I always brought peanuts with me to the park. I'd feed them to my pal, Liam the squirrel, and his friends. Now he would have to starve because of me. I felt terrible for letting Liam down.

Ah, but faithful Liam still came by to say hello. At least "he" liked me. Then all of a sudden it was like a dam burst. I started crying so hard I couldn't stop. All I could think about was how much trouble I was going to be in for running away.

I looked up at a big oak tree near me and watched the squirrels through my tears. They reminded me of how my mind felt. It was jumping from thought to thought like the squirrels jumping from branch to branch. Oh my, I really did have Restless Brain Syndrome. I wondered if the squirrels had it too?

Then something happened I didn't expect. Through my tears I noticed someone walking toward me on the path near my bench. It was some dude wearing a funny costume and it wasn't even Halloween! He didn't dress like anyone I knew, that was for sure. I wondered if he was a space alien from another galaxy.

I quickly looked away as he got closer. I pretended I didn't see him. Once he passed by, I turned around.

He was wearing something that kind of looked like a red bathrobe. He was all wrapped up in it. This needed some checking out for sure! For protection I made myself invisible using my secret powers.

I sniffled and wiped my tears. I climbed down off the bench real slow once he was far enough away.

I didn't get far. Before I knew it, he stopped, turned around, and faced me. My eyes almost popped out of my head. "Oh no! It's Tenzin!" What was Tenzin doing here in the park?! This was double doom. I couldn't think. I couldn't speak. I froze like a deer in the headlights.

"Hello, Mitchell!" Tenzin is Betsy's friend from Tibet. She helps him practice his English from time to time. Obviously he had psychic powers too 'cause he knew I was behind him the whole time.

I put my hands into my pockets. I started whistling a made-up song so he wouldn't suspect anything. I started to get nervous. Would Tenzin rat me out?

Finally I said, "Why are you dressed so funny? What's up with that, Tenzin?"

This made him start laughing. You see, whenever Tenzin came by our house he dressed normal. He wore jeans and a button-down shirt. I've never seen him dressed like this before.

"These are my monk's robes, Mitchell; I don't always wear them here in the city because they are very special."

"Oh yeah, interesting." MONKS? Like I even knew what that meant. I did know Tenzin was a real nice fellow. He always talked to me and was friendly when he would visit our home. A couple of times he even played Legos with me. Betsy liked him a lot. She thought he was real nice and special. But...I sure didn't know what this MONKS thing was. I didn't know what he was talking about.

I just figured he was part of some secret underground organization controlled by chimps! I needed to get to the bottom of this.

"Tenzin, what's a MONKS?"

Tenzin's pet yak in Tibet.

by Mitchell Hoffsteader

Tenzin told me he became a *MONK* when he was as small as me. He grew up and lived in a monastery with other monks. The monastery was in Tibet. That's where he got the special robes to wear. I asked Tenzin if a monastery was like a monk hotel.

I knew about Tibet…I learned about it in school. It's next to China and India where the Himalaya mountains are. I liked Tenzin's monk robes. He looked cool in them.

Tenzin said he had a question for me. "WHY are you in the park by yourself and not in school?" Fear zoomed through my body and my palms got sweaty. Now I was in the hot seat!

I didn't know what to do. I knew it was bad to lie so I confessed to Tenzin, "Uh, well, I had to take the day off because I have a severe case of Restless Brain Syndrome."

"Restless WHAT?" asked Tenzin.

"RESTLESS BRAIN SYNDROME!" I shouted. "Doesn't anyone know about Restless Brain Syndrome!? You know, when you can't stop thinking and thinking."

"Oh, I see, well I hope you feel better real soon, Mitchell."

"Yeah, I hope so too," I sadly replied.

"Tenzin, what do monks do? What do you do for fun?"

Tenzin said, with an extra big smile I might add, that he studies and practices Tibetan medicine. That's because he likes to help people. He also likes to meditate and study the teachings of the Buddha.

"Maybe you should learn to *MEDITATE*, Mitchell. It might help you with your Restless Brain Syndrome. Meditation helps my mind stay peaceful and happy."

"*MEDICATE?* NO no no!!!" I shouted.

"*MEDITATE*," Tenzin said, laughing.

"Oh, that's a different story. What IS meditate?"

Tenzin got all serious. He told me that doing meditation helps all kinds of people. It helps them to have a more peaceful mind and better concentration.

"Meditating helps us become more *MINDFUL*. When we are mindful we live more in the present moment." I didn't really understand what he was talking about. Tenzin noticed I was starting to get antsy.

Very calmly he said, "Paying attention to whatever we are doing in the moment is being mindful, Mitchell. Practicing meditation helps us find the peacefulness inside ourselves. When we are peaceful and calm we become happier, more accepting, and content."

"Ohhhhhh." That made a little sense to me.

He assured me that meditation was not new; it has been around for thousands of years.

Tenzin said and I quote, "*Don't worry Mitchell. EVERYONE EVERYWHERE has Restless Brain Syndrome from time to time.* Even me. I've had it."

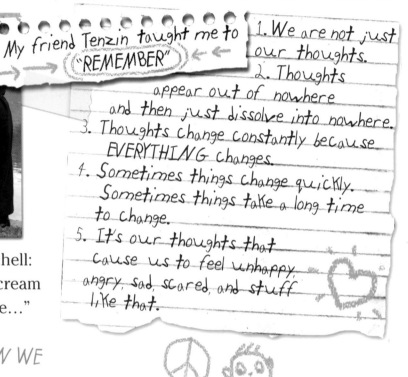

My friend Tenzin taught me to "REMEMBER"

1. We are not just our thoughts.
2. Thoughts appear out of nowhere and then just dissolve into nowhere.
3. Thoughts change constantly because EVERYTHING changes.
4. Sometimes things change quickly. Sometimes things take a long time to change.
5. It's our thoughts that cause us to feel unhappy, angry, sad, scared, and stuff like that.

"Think about this, Mitchell: suppose I had vanilla ice cream and gave it to three people…"

"ICE CREAM! HAND DIPPED? TENZIN, CAN WE GO FOR ICE CREAM?"

"Mitchell, are you LISTENING?"

"Yes, noooo, well a little."

"Okay, then suppose I gave some of the same ice cream to each one of them. Maybe two people would eat it and say, 'YUM, I love this vanilla ice cream!' Then one person would say, 'YUCK, take it away, I don't like this vanilla ice cream at all.' But they all tasted the very same vanilla ice cream. So you can see, everyone reacts differently because of their thoughts. Even trickier, HOW we react to our thoughts determines how we feel about things and even ourselves.

This is important to remember, Mitchell."

I wondered how Tenzin knew all of this. Maybe he really was from another planet. Nah, I kind of did understand what he was talking about a little; I just never really had anyone explain it to me. Tenzin said something that kind of puzzled me though. He said, "Our minds make us feel unhappy because of their habit of attachment."

When Tenzin said "attachment" I rolled my eyes...What was he talking about now — attachment?

Tenzin caught me rolling my eyes, and laughed. Then he rolled his eyes, which really made me laugh. Tenzin can be pretty funny sometimes. Tenzin told me to, "Think of attachment as a sticky-gluey-clingy thought. We cling onto wanting things to be or go a certain way. That's because we believe it will make us feel good. It's like we get hooked on thinking about something and can't stop. Then it's hard for us to get unstuck. It's difficult for us to think clearly. That's when the trouble begins for us, Mitchell. When things we desire and want don't happen the way we would like, we start to feel upset. We can become mad, fearful, or a lot of things."

What Tenzin said got me thinking. Every day at school I sat in the blue chair at the lunch table. Each day I expected to have MY seat.

One day third-grader Thomas was sitting there innocently eating his lunch. The fiend! I got mad because he was in the seat I wanted! My mind was all clingy and stuck on having the blue chair to sit in when I wanted it. Truth was, Thomas was just enjoying his cheese sandwich. Thomas sniffled a lot but he was a nice kid.

"Sometimes we try to push away uncomfortable thoughts, feelings, and situations. We think doing so will make us feel better and happier. When stuff doesn't change as fast as we want, we get frustrated and feel worse."

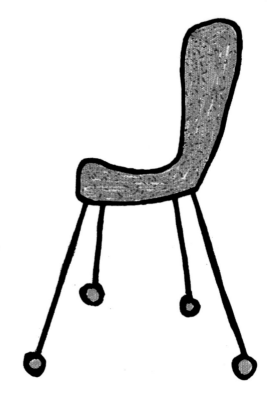

This made me think again of when Thomas would not move out of _MY_ blue chair. I felt angry inside because things did not go the way I wanted. My thoughts were glued to having the chair when I wanted it. My anger seemed to get worse because I could not control it. I couldn't stop it. I kept on thinking over and over how Thomas took _MY_ chair. The harder I tried to stop thinking about what Thomas did, the stickier and worse my thoughts got. I got madder and madder. Then I got angry and disappointed in myself for not being able to stop my anger.

"Did you ever notice, Mitchell, how most of the time we are thinking about the past or future, instead of being in the present moment? For instance, we eat fast and don't really taste the food because we are thinking of something else."

"Oh yeahhhhh, kind of like when I turn into Captain Space Out!" I declared.

Boy, I think I must confuse Tenzin sometimes. Because he looked really puzzled when he asked me, "Who's Captain Space Out?" I wiggled my eyebrows and made a big grin at Tenzin. He got it because he laughed. "Anyway, Mitchell, we aren't being mindful. We are on automatic pilot. Remember, being mindful is when you are calmly aware and paying attention to whatever you are experiencing and doing in the moment. You don't put a positive or negative value on it. Even yourself, Mitchell. Reacting with judgement and being critical can cause you to

experience unpleasant feelings like self doubt, anger and unhappiness."

I asked Tenzin if, by reacting, he meant the way we like or dislike something. "A-f-f-i-r-m-a-t-i-v-e," he spelled, "which is a big fat *YES*."

I remembered how I didn't like Thomas sitting in the blue chair. Maybe I could have had *unsticky, unjudgie* thoughts, you know, calm-kind thoughts instead. I could have wisely realized that some days I will get the blue chair and some days I won't. FACT: the blue chair is for everyone to share, even Thomas. FACT: I AM HAPPY FOR THOMAS. That is the truth and knowing that makes me feel better. It's not because Thomas was being mean to me. He deserved to sit there too.

AND NOW FOR A COMMERCIAL BREAK!

For An Unlimited Time – Always...MINDFULNESS

1. FRIENDS, are you tired of eating so fast you don't really taste your food?
2. Do your parents or friends often say, *"HELLO? ARE YOU LISTENING TO ME?"*
3. Does your mind DRIFT when you read?
   Do you REMEMBER what you read?

TO TRY A FREE SAMPLE OF MINDFULNESS — DO THE FOLLOWING:

Sit comfortably and gently close your eyes. Become aware of your body. How does your body feel while you are sitting?

Place your hand on your belly. Can you feel your belly move in and out from breathing? Feel your hand on your belly. Feel your clothing against your hand. Really become aware of how it feels.

Begin to feel your feet. Do they feel heavy, warm, tingly? Can you feel what you are sitting on? What do you sense?

Feel both your hands. Pay attention to how your hands feel. Do your hands feel thick, itchy, prickly?

Be mindful of your ears. How do both your ears feel? Are they warm, tingly, buzzing?

Maybe your ears are hearing sounds. Just notice the sounds. How do the insides of your ears feel?

Now bring your awareness to your eyeballs. Mindfully feel your eyeballs. Now feel your eyelids. Slowly and mindfully open your eyes.

Free! Free! Free!

YOU HAVE BEEN MINDFUL!

MINDFULNESS
MINDFULNESS
MINDFULNESS
yours FREE with
NO monthly down payments
NO high-interest rates

AND don't forget...

Mindfully hold this book. How does the book feel in your hands? Really be aware of how the book feels!

How does the paper feel against your fingers? Notice the color and texture of the paper.

Look mindfully at the words. *Oh, you are so mindful!*

READY, SET, GO...BACK TO TENZIN!

I asked Tenzin if we could go to the stream in the park. I liked the stream because it was fun stepping on the stones in the water. When we got there Tenzin told me to pay attention to the water. "See how the water looks, Mitchell?" I used my X-ray vision to look. I didn't see what the big deal was. Tenzin pointed and told me to focus on the water. "The water looks like it stays the same, but really it is changing all the time."

"Mitchell, when we understand in our hearts that all things change, especially our thoughts, we will live a lot easier. It really is best to accept thoughts to be just what they are — just thoughts — and let them come and go."

"The thoughts that make you feel truly happy, peaceful, and loving toward yourself and others, Mitchell, are the ones to pay attention to and trust."

From my meditation journal!

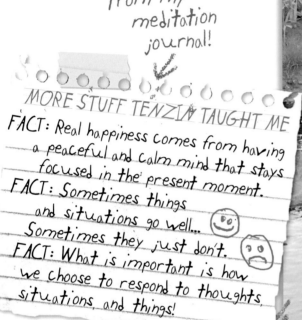

MORE STUFF TENZIN TAUGHT ME

FACT: Real happiness comes from having a peaceful and calm mind that stays focused in the present moment.

FACT: Sometimes things and situations go well... Sometimes they just don't.

FACT: What is important is how we choose to respond to thoughts, situations, and things!

I really thought about what Tenzin said. It kind of made sense to me. Tenzin really got me thinking in a wiser way!

We kept looking at the stream together so we could really watch how the water was changing.

We looked at the sky. I told Tenzin how I thought my mind was like the sky sometimes.

"Tenzin, you know how the sky can be sunny and blue? Well sometimes my mind feels sunny with happy thoughts. But, here's the big BUT...dark clouds float through my Mitchell sky mind. The dark clouds are there when I am mad, lonely, sad, scared, and stuff like that."

"I think there's a lot of precipitation going on in my head, Tenzin. Sometimes the dark clouds never seem to want to go away. They really make me feel bad."

As usual, Tenzin had something wise and helpful to say. "Look at the clouds in the sky. See how they are moving and changing even as we talk? Remember, Mitchell, everything

changes. Now there is blue sky peeking through."

What really made me think was when Tenzin told me, "Sometimes our minds get in the habit of having negative dark-cloud thoughts and reactions. We start to believe them. The same way clouds cover up the sunny blue sky, negative thoughts cover up our happy peaceful mind. Meditation helps us realize that negative thoughts are just thoughts too — they are not necessarily true."

I wondered if negative thoughts were the same as "monster thoughts." I told Tenzin all about my monster thoughts and how I didn't like them at all. He said that monster thoughts were for sure the same as negative thoughts, and they are not true at all. Boy did that make me happy! Tenzin told me to trust my buddy thoughts.

"Mitchell, you really can train your mind so it has better concentration and awareness. You can train your mind to stay more in the present moment and have less gluey-sticky thoughts. You can teach it to have more loving, kind, and peaceful thoughts too. Meditation can help with all of this."

Before long, a lot of what Tenzin was saying started to make sense to me. I noticed I was feeling better too. How do you like that? I was having happier thoughts and feeling better. I was changing!

WOW, TENZIN SURE IS DEEP! Now I knew Tenzin was right. I was becoming more aware of my thoughts, and how they made me feel. I was noticing how my thoughts were changing. Sometimes I had sad or scary thoughts. Sometimes I had angry thoughts. A lot of times I had funny and happy thoughts. I liked feeding Liam the squirrel. That was a happy, loving buddy thought!

Liam

by Mitchell H.

I started to think maybe my Restless Brain Syndrome wasn't so bad after all. That was a thought. What seemed to make having Restless Brain Syndrome worse were my own thoughts about having it.

I'd been thinking I was broken inside. I thought I was an unlovable little fellow for having Restless Brain Syndrome, which wasn't true at all. You see, I hadn't been telling myself very nice things. I was believing all those monster thoughts about me. Oh, how tricky my mind could be.

So you know what I did? I asked Tenzin if he could please teach me to meditate. He said, "Yes," if Betsy said it was okay.

I thanked Tenzin in backwards talk for helping me feel better. "!SKNAHT" I waved goodbye and took off like a rocket toward home.

Tomorrow would be a big day!

I was going to learn how to meditate! Hooray! I ran as fast as I could, taking shortcuts all the way home.

I made it home fast! When I got to the front door of my house I froze like a popsicle. I remembered how much trouble I was going to be in for running away. I could hardly breathe. I couldn't move. Somehow I had to sneak back into my room without Betsy catching me. With all my might I made my legs move. The door didn't squeak or make a sound when I pushed it open. I was lucky. I tiptoed into the house.

I was almost safely back in my bedroom when I heard the voice of doom fill the air. A cold chill ran down my spine. It was Betzilla! She heard me come in with her supersonic hearing. "MITCHELL, WHERE HAVE YOU BEEN?!" Flames and smoke were shooting out of her mouth. "I have been looking for you everywhere!"

Betzilla!

My stomach flip-flopped. I hung my head, avoiding eye contact. I held back my tears. I could hardly open my mouth to speak. "I ran away to the park because of my Restless Brain Syndrome and that's the truth," I mumbled.

"Your Restless WHAT Syndrome? Don't you EVER do that again!" Then Betsy's voice softened, "I was worried sick."

Before my human controller commanded me, I went straight to my designated time-out corner to be tortured and think about what I did wrong. Once I was in my corner I started to whimper. I couldn't help it. Betzilla would make me stand there until I turned into a pile of dust.

Then a miracle happened. As I stood there disintegrating, Betzilla came over and gave me a big hug. What was this? *A HUG?* Had Betzilla come to her senses? I guess she really was worried about me. Anyway, I knew she was right about my running away. It was not a good thing to do at all. I promised from my heart I'd never run away again.

Chapter 3

I Did It.
I Learned
To Meditate!

The next day I got up super early because I was so excited! Tenzin was coming by after school to teach me how to meditate. Betsy thought it was okay. In fact she thought it was a real good idea!

When Tenzin showed up he was wearing his special monk's robes again. It was neat.

Betsy made us tea to drink, because Tenzin likes tea. Tenzin and I sat on the living-room floor to drink our tea and to meditate. He said I could sit anywhere I wanted to meditate as long as I was comfortable.

For starters, Tenzin explained to me that there were many kinds of meditation, just like there were many kinds of languages. He said he was going to teach me how to do *MINDFUL BREATH MEDITATION*.

"HUH?" *BREATH* meditation? What does BREATH have to do with meditation? Breathing? No way! "Meditation can't be just about breathing. Is it magical breath, Tenzin?"

"Yes, BREATHING. All you are going to do, Mitchell, is pay attention to your breath as you are sitting here."

"My breath? Really?" Who would have known? "Sounds easy peasy to me." Truth was, I never even noticed my breath before.

"Tenzin is a pretty smart dude."

Before we started, we read a little about meditation and why it is good to do. Tenzin's book explained that *ANYONE* could meditate and receive its benefits. "Even someone like me with a bad case of Restless Brain Syndrome?" I wondered. What good news!

To guide me through meditation, first Tenzin asked me to shut my eyes. Then he calmly told me to start paying attention to my breathing. "See if you can notice your belly going in and out each time you breathe." I did. I could actually feel my belly go in and out as I was breathing. After awhile Tenzin asked me to notice the breath going in and out of my nose. "Don't force it to be stronger, deeper, or faster. Just allow your breath to go in and out naturally. See if you can notice one in and one out breath, Mitchell." I tried doing what Tenzin told me to do.

"Mitchell, pretend your awareness is like a flashlight. Shine the bright light of your flashlight awareness directly on your breath. Shine it so you can really notice your breath. You might even still notice your belly going in and out from breathing. That's okay too, Mitchell."

I tried with all my might to pay real close attention to my breath. I shined my flashlight awareness on it. Sometimes I did feel my belly moving in and out. It seemed easy for about a second. Then something happened I didn't expect. All of a sudden, for no reason, my mind started thinking about everything but my breath. It wouldn't stay focused on my breath. I couldn't concentrate.

What was going on? What was wrong? All of a sudden I realized I was fantasizing about chocolate brownie batter. I licked it out of the mixing bowl three days ago after Betsy made me brownies. My mouth started to water. Mmmmm, I could almost taste the gooey brownie batter again. Then I started to remember about how I forgot to feed my pet hermit crab, Cornelius, this morning. I began to worry he might starve. What was happening? My mind kept wandering. I couldn't control my thinking. My mind kept jumping from thought to thought. It didn't want to behave and listen to me at all.

Suddenly I heard Tenzin say, "If your mind wanders off, Mitchell, calmly bring it back to your breathing. Don't get mad or frustrated. Be real kind toward yourself. Bring your awareness back to your breath. You can do it."

Oh boy, it was pretty obvious that my mind was wandering. That was it — now I was going to get real serious! No more thinking about brownie batter or weak, starving Cornelius for me. I was going to observe my breath.

"Patiently keep bringing your attention back to your breath each time it wanders off." But by the time I heard him say "wanders" I started to notice how itchy my nose was. I wanted to scratch it so bad, I almost couldn't stand it anymore. It was torture. I tried real hard not to scratch it.

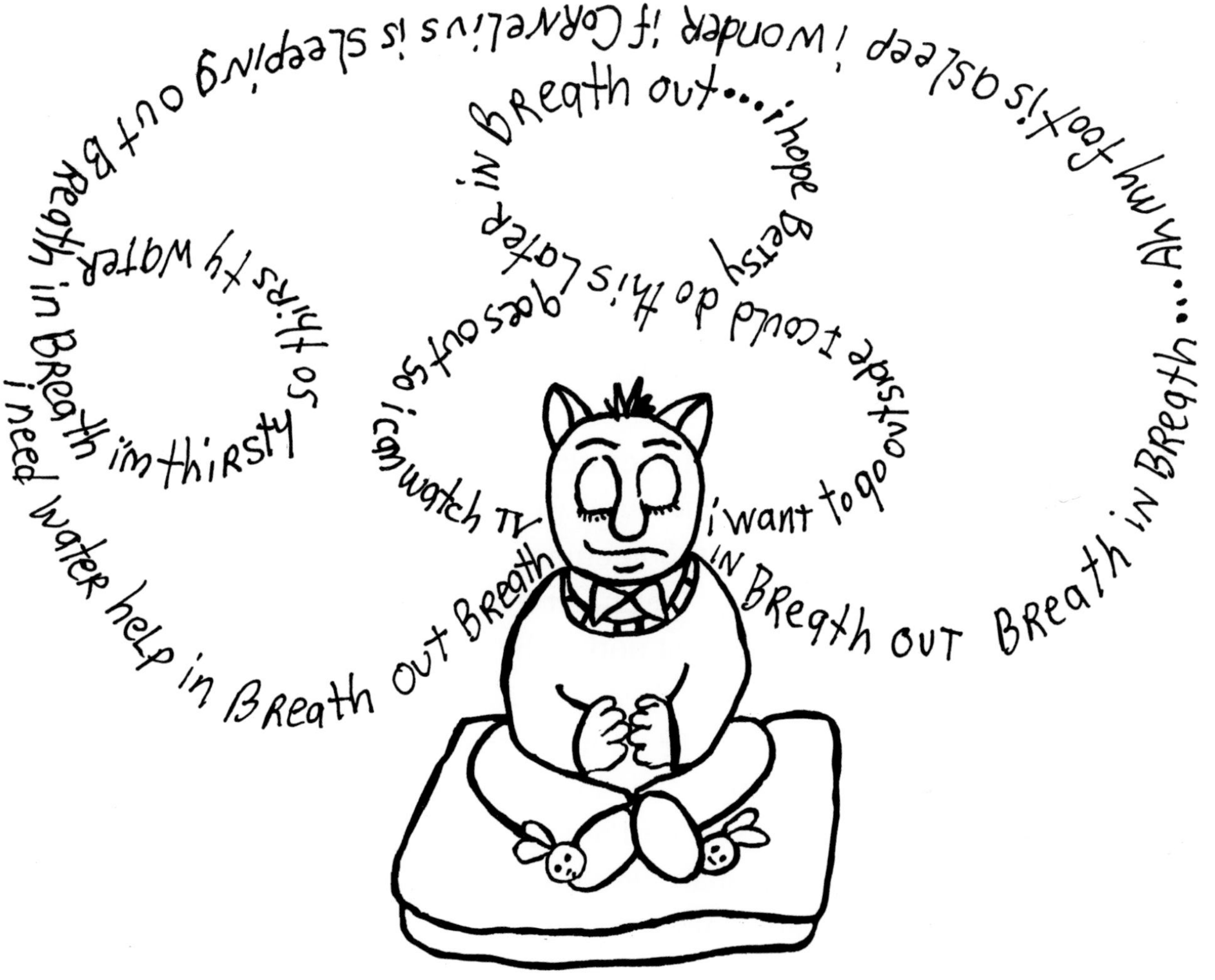

I realized I was not paying attention to my breath. I kept focusing on my itchy nose. I was hoping it would stop itching.

ALL OF A SUDDEN IT WAS LIKE A LIGHT BULB WENT ON IN MY HEAD! I REALIZED I WAS NOT MEDITATING! I WAS NOT PAYING ATTENTION TO MY BREATH AT ALL.

So as best as I could, without getting frustrated, I calmly brought my attention back to my breath. My mind still kept trying to wander. Each time I caught it wandering I'd give it a little tug and bring it back to my breath. In, out, in, out went my breath.

Magically, I no longer wanted to scratch my nose. Instead I was just being aware of my breath. In it came and out it went. I could actually feel the breath passing in and out of my nostrils. Sometimes it felt fuzzy and warm and sometimes it seemed cool. Once I even felt a tickle below my nose. I never felt that before. I allowed myself to just notice the tickling feeling, then I went right back to observing my breath. I kept on trying.

My mind kept on trying to think about lots of things. I had a parade of thoughts marching through my head. Sometimes the thoughts in the parade were so loud and colorful it was hard not to march along with them. Whenever I'd catch myself thinking and marching along, I'd jump out of the parade just by noticing my breath again. I did not give up. I was actually starting to like my Mitchell mind.

As I sat there I became more mindful of how my body felt sitting. It felt heavy. I was aware of my hands and legs like never before.

I could feel the cushion I was sitting on. It was squishy. Then I went back to paying attention to my breath.

At one point, as I was meditating, something really neat happened. My mind began to feel calm and less jumpy. I was just paying attention to my breathing. I was not thinking about anything else.

My mind was in the *PRESENT MOMENT.* I was only noticing my breath. My Mitchell mind

seemed calmer and more focused. I felt good.

How do you like that? "I am pretty good," I thought. Meditating was fun! Oops, I caught myself thinking about how much fun meditation was. I realized I just had to go back to paying attention to my breath.

Finally, Tenzin asked me to open my eyes.

When I did I was smiling without even trying. I felt different but in a good way. I felt relaxed and my mind was not racing with thoughts. I didn't feel like a scatterbrain anymore. My mind felt less scrambled. I didn't feel wobbly and restless inside either. I felt peaceful and quiet inside like never before.

"That's meditation?" What fun! *"MEDITATION IS GOOD FOR ME!"*

Tenzin was smiling because he was really happy for me. "Yes, that is meditation and you, Mitchell, have meditated. Remember, peacefulness is always there; meditating will help you find it."

We both clapped and then I shouted really loud to Betsy, "I MEDITATED!" Betsy was so happy she came and gave me a big bear hug. That made me feel special.

Tenzin assured me that anyone anywhere could meditate. It didn't matter if they were young or old. It didn't matter if they wore tube socks or no socks. Or what religion they were or weren't. Anyone could benefit from meditation.

"I know why, Tenzin! Everyone breathes, everyone everywhere. So if they are breathing, they could practice mindful breath meditation."

"We are all the same, right, Tenzin? Just like everyone has Restless Brain Syndrome from time to time, everyone can have a calmer, more loving, and more peaceful mind too."

"Yes, Mitchell, we ARE all the same. All living beings want to be peaceful and happy — that is universal. By 'universal' I mean everywhere on the planet. Even places we are not able to see or are not aware of. We are all part of this wonderful magical universe."

"That means we are magical and wonderful too, Tenzin?"

"Yes, Mitchell!"

MEDITATION IS FOR ME!

"Maybe if I light up from the inside out like a lantern, with happiness and peace, others will feel it. I'd be helping others feel happier and more peaceful."

"Yes again, Mitchell. They will start to sense and feel it."

may all beings be safe

share peace, share love, share happiness

have fun meditating   kind and caring

trust your feelings and heart

may all beings be safe and happy

peaceful as a rainbow

trust your feelings and heart

share peace, share love, share happiness

happy as a butterfly

everything changes

happy as a butterfly   be mindful

have fun meditating

in breath out breath   just be   share peace, share love, share happiness

attention and awareness

thoughts constantly change

peaceful as a rainbow   be happy   present moment   everything changes

be peaceful

Chapter 4

Really,
Anyone Can Meditate

Me and my buddy Tenzin still take walks and talk. We talk about lots of stuff like how to play with finger puppets, why polar bears are white, AND how I'd like to have a brown pony.

Tenzin even helped me find replacement ants for my new and improved glass-encased ant farm! We like watching the ants together, even though they're pretty boring as usual. I still learn lots about meditation from Tenzin too. We talk about it a lot because I still have lots of questions.

May all brown ponies be loved and happy

You know what? Betsy even wanted to learn how to meditate, so I taught her how. Now Betsy and I meditate together. We meditate every day! We meditate together every morning and at night before I go to bed.

The neat thing is, I can meditate anywhere because my breath goes with me everywhere. I like to meditate when I ride in the car or when I ride on the bus. When kids are jumping around and screaming on the bus and the driver yells, "Shut up and sit down!" *I MEDITATE.* If I don't have lots of time I only meditate for a minute or so. Like maybe five minutes. When I have time I like to meditate for sixteen minutes because sixteen is my favorite number.

NEWS FLASH: I now have friends!

I learned that other kids really do like me and want to be my friend. I taught my friends how to meditate. Sometimes we play together. Sometimes we meditate together. Kids at school call me MINDFUL MITCHIE! I really don't feel like an outsider anymore. You know what too? *I noticed the more I practice meditating, the more my Restless Brain Syndrome seems to fade away!*

Sure, I still get angry, disappointed, and scared sometimes. Monster thoughts still try to sneak up on me, but now my buddy thoughts chase them away. I can still be a little *persnickety,* according to Betsy and Miss Millmont. I guess I am like everyone else. I just try to remember that they are old habits, my old ways of acting. They are not the real me. Meditation helps me understand that. I do my best to be as mindful and accepting of them as I can, because they are not permanent.

I try hard not to judge myself too.

The easier I am on myself, the better I feel. When I experience tough thoughts and emotions, I try to be extra kind and caring to myself.

I'm learning that my own peacefulness and happiness depend a lot on my Hoffsteader attitude towards things.

FACT:
Now I wear my safety helmet!
I know it's important to do because I want to take care of myself.

49

I try to be kind to everyone. I am even careful not to step on bugs. I don't want to harm them or others!

I like being kind and helpful to others these days. When I am, I can tell it makes them happy. It's kind of fun helping out. I keep my room cleaner too. Betsy lets me vacuum...a lot! Whenever I want to see Betsy faint, I just clean my room!

Remember how I used to worry about the polar bears? Now I help them. Instead of worrying, I donate some of my weekly allowance that Banker Betsy gives me to help protect polar bears. I plant trees and recycle to help my friend, planet Earth. I am an official Hoffsteader helper bee.

What's really cool is I have a lot more buddy thoughts these days! My buddy thoughts are all the nice things I think about myself. My faithful buddy thoughts always make me feel happy and confident. One thing I have learned is that it's really good to talk to someone about my worries, fears, sadness, and anger. When I do, I feel better.

I like being Kind & helpful!

NEWS FLASH! I haven't been in my time-out corner for a long time. Now there are cobweb condos there and the spiders are my friends. AND...I don't tell Betsy she should go stand in her own time-out corner anymore! Betsy says she's real proud of me now that I am meditating. She says meditation is helping me become more patient. She likes that I don't inhale my food like a vacuum cleaner at meals anymore. I'm as mindful as I can be when I eat. My food tastes better too. Even vegetables!

NEWS FLASH! Good ole Miss Millmont says my grades are getting better since I've been meditating. She also says I don't disrupt class as much either. She likes that I am calmer. It's probably because I have an easier time concentrating when I'm in class. I stay a lot calmer even when I take stinky, boring, "*YAWN*" multiplication tests. I just try and do my best!

You know what? It's easier for me to evoke the aesthetic simplicity of the curvaceous macaroni when I create mindfully. Observe how the macaroni boldly radiates in the composition of a free-standing pencil holder. My macaroni art projects are totally da Vinci! I try my best to be mindful Mitchie. I'm mindful when I'm studying, eating cereal, reading, and experimenting in my secret lab.

AND...one thing is for sure, meditation helps me think more with my ♥.

So now all you earthlings can see that practicing meditation helps me a lot...I am still Mitchell, but I'm a happier and more peaceful Mitchell!

1ST PRIZE

Thank you Meditation, My Friend... THE END

Chapter 5

I Forgot to Mention...

...how Tenzin taught me to do loving kindness meditation. It's called Metta. Metta's fun and very good to do. It's now one of my official superpowers! Metta's when you send kind and loving thoughts to yourself and others. When I do it, I pretend I am sending invisible hugs. I usually do Metta before I go to bed at night. I do it after I do my breath meditation.

Here are some of the things I think to myself when I do Metta. "May I, Mitchell, be safe and free from harm.

May I be content.

May I be as peaceful as a fluffy white cloud.

May I, Mitchell, be as happy as a butterfly and laugh a lot.

May I share my Legos and other toys."

Then I send myself a big hug. That makes me feel warm and fuzzy inside. I feel pretty special.

That's me using my superpower Metta before bed.

I always say to myself, "May I share my happiness, peace, and love with everybody I meet."

Then I think the same good thoughts for Betsy, Tenzin, and my friends. Sometimes I even send Metta to someone who has made me mad like Walter Patuziak, the skunk. Walter's okay, and I know skunks want to be happy too.

I always send Metta to the noble ants in my ant farm. I send them thoughts like, "May all the little ants — Edwin, Peepo, Effy, Cecil, and Jingles — be happy. May all the tiny ants at my ant farm be free from harm in their new home. May all the ants have enough food to eat."

Edwin

Peepo

Effy

Cecil

Jingles

So you see, you can be pretty creative with Metta. You can send Metta vibes to anyone you like. For fun, I send it to people I don't even know.

I think that everybody everywhere wants to be peaceful and happy. I like to send Metta to people who are sick, and to people who have no food to eat. Once I even sent it to all people everywhere who have the same birthday as Betsy and me. I know they want to be happy. AND I send Metta to planet Earth and to polar bears. I send it to as many animals as I can!

Here are some ideas of what you can say
when you do "Mighty Metta"

May all beings* be free from pain and suffering.

May all beings be safe and free from harm.

May all beings live with ease.

May all beings be peaceful and happy.

May they be loved.

May I share my peace, love, and happiness with
all beings everywhere.

* By "beings" I mean people, babies, plants, fish, birds, whales,
all animals, bugs, stars, anyone, and everything!

Chapter 6

Look
Who Meditates

I meet all kinds of people who meditate.

Look who meditates!

Yun, the Artist, Meditates

Firefighter Anthony Meditates

Big Jim, the Systems Analyst, Meditates

Yep, anyone can meditate!

Gail,
the Gardener,
Meditates

Nurse Ann
Marie
Meditates

Mr. Alosi,
the Tourist,
Meditates

Surprise: even kids meditate!

Twins
Meditate

Anyone can meditate!

Kids who skate and
love pink Meditate

Kids who love
sports Meditate

METTA MEDITATION

MEDITATION INSTRUCTIONS

2. If your mind wanders off, gently bring it back to your breath.

E. A nice thing to do before you finish doing Metta is to say to yourself, "May I share my happiness with everyone everywhere."

A. It is best to practice Metta when you are calm and relaxed and not in a hurry.

1. Find a nice comfortable sitting position.

1. Meditation is fun
2. You can do it
3. Give it a try
4. You are a Meditator

D. Now you can do Metta for others.

C. Once you are sitting to meditate, mindfully become aware of your body.

3. See if you can bring your awareness to your breath.

METTA MEDITATION

METTA MEDITATION

4. You can meditate as long as you like.

MEDITATION INSTRUCTIONS

B. Become aware of your in breath and your out breath.

F. Don't forget, with Metta you can be as creative as you like.

Special
Meditation Instructions

Betsy helped me a lot on this chapter.

BREATH MEDITATION

One thing I've learned is that when you meditate it's really important not to expect special things to happen. Just try your best. It's not about being perfect. Let your meditation experience unfold and flow naturally. Just see what happens. JUST BE with whatever YOU experience.

1. Find a cozy, comfortable sitting position. I sit on my meditation cushion on the floor except when I meditate in bed at night. Red alert! Don't lie down when you meditate. I did. Then I fell asleep and started to snore. It's cool if you create a special meditation space in your home where you practice. Mine has peaceful, happy Hoffsteader vibes from all my meditating and Metta!

2. Start meditating by paying attention to how your body feels as you are sitting. What are YOU aware of? What do YOU notice? Don't overthink it. Who knows? You might sense warmth, heaviness, or what you are sitting on. Maybe you'll notice how your clothes feel touching your body. Maybe you won't notice anything at all. How does it feel just to be sitting? Remember, whatever you sense and notice is fine because it's what's true and happening for YOU in the moment. If you want you can take a few "done-on-purpose breaths." Keeping your mouth closed, breathe in slowly, sending the breath right down to your toes. Then exhale slowly through your nose. Doing this before you meditate can help calm and steady your mind if it is real jumpy.

3. Next, bring your attention to your breathing. Relax and become aware of your body as you breathe. What does that feel like? Is your chest moving as you breathe? Is your belly going in and out? Can you hear your breathing? Just be mindful of your breathing. Now pay attention to your nose. How does your nose feel, inside and out, as you breathe? See if you can notice breath going in and out of your nose. Try your best to pay attention to one in breath, and then one out breath.

Don't force your breathing; let your breath flow naturally. Just be mindful of what it's doing. JUST BE with your breathing. (Imagine you saw a butterfly resting on a flower. You think, "Ahhh, a butterfly." Now see if you can use the same amount of enthusiasm, curiosity, and attention you have with the butterfly on your breath. Nice and easy, but with enthusiasm. Ahhhh, breath.) JUST BE mindful of your breath. Try not to get discouraged when your mind wanders. Patiently and calmly bring your attention back to your breathing. Just begin over and over, with patience toward yourself. "I, Mitchie, can say for sure that I have to start over and over again a lot, but I don't mind. I know it's okay. I just keep practicing and trying." Before you're done meditating and you open your eyes, see if you can notice stillness and quietness inside yourself.

4. You know what? You can meditate as long as you like. Give yourself comfortable goals that you know you can handle when you meditate. You can meditate for a minute, five or ten minutes, or even more. You decide. Practicing meditation every day is the key. The more you practice, the better you'll get the hang of it. You'll see. Oh yeah, if you ever have to shift your position while you are meditating like I do sometimes, remember, do it mindfully.

5. One thing I've noticed is that some days it seems easier than others to meditate. Sometimes everything goes okay. My concentration is good. It is easy to be mindful of my breath. Other days I can hardly sit still to meditate. It's like

Peepo and Jingles are crawling around in my pants! I don't feel like meditating at all. But I still try my best. I still meditate. Then that changes. Because, as you know, everything changes. Even how a meditation sit goes.

Don't grade yourself as a meditator or your meditation sits. Don't think bad or good. What's important is how you treat yourself and relate to the thoughts you have as you meditate. Be kind to yourself.

Be your own BFF. AND, remember, have fun meditating!

HOW TO DO MIGHTY METTA

Trust your ♥ and feelings about who to send Metta to and what to say. You can send it to friends, family, neighbors, all animals, anything, or anyone. Don't forget, it's important to send Metta to yourself! 😊

Doing Metta after breath meditation is a good idea. It is best to do when you are calm and not in a hurry.

1. *Imagine you are holding someone or something you really care about in your lap, like a baby or a pet or any animal.* You can imagine an animal you love even if you don't have pets. I like to pretend I am holding Liam in my lap. Next, tap into the good feelings you have for whomever you are holding there. See if you can let the feelings of love and happiness you have for them fill up your entire body. Let the Metta vibes float into your toes, legs, fingers, arms, belly, and head. Let the Metta vibes radiate and sparkle throughout your body. For fun, try imagining a golden, white, or pink light radiating throughout your entire body. Any color you like. Keep sending the good feelings, vibrations, and colors of love to whomever is sitting in your lap. Think and send thoughts like this to them:

   Be loved, _Liam_. Be peaceful, _Liam_. Be happy, _Liam_.

2. *Next, try imagining your sister, brother, or your mom or dad, or a relative or friend, or anyone you like sitting in front of you.* Let the feelings, vibrations, and colors of love and happiness grow in your heart and fill up your body again. Send it out to whomever you imagine is sitting in front of you. Trust yourself on what to say. Use thoughts that work best for you!

You can also try using the thoughts below as you send the Metta.

I wish for _____ to be peaceful. I wish for _____ to be loved.

I wish for _____ to be happy.

3. *Now that you have the hang of it, try sending Metta to yourself.*
Remember this is really important! Connect with the feelings, vibrations, and colors of love and joy in your heart. Let them radiate, sparkle, and go everywhere throughout your entire body. Imagine yourself surrounded by these sparkly vibrations. Let these vibrations of Metta beam right out of you. While you send yourself Metta, try saying this silently:

May__*I*__be peaceful.

May__*I*__be loved.

May__*I*__be happy.

May__*I*__share my peace, happiness, and love with everyone everywhere.

Other things I like to say: May I help others. May I be grateful. May I be a good friend to myself and others. May I be a good student. May I be kind and caring.

Fun Things
To Do With
Meditation

Fun Things To Do With

Have an official meditation sleepover.

- **Invite meditation buddies over and put on cool pj's.**

- **Have lots of good snacks to eat. But not sugary ones** or nobody will be able to sit still and meditate! For fun, try eating one special snack in silence, but mindfully.

- **Build a secret meditation hut.** Use four chairs and cover them over with blankets. You can use flashlights inside.

- **On a piece of paper, have each person write someone's name they would like to have Metta said for.** Put the names in a bowl. Have each meditator select one and say the name out loud to the others. These names can be included when everybody does Metta.

Meditation hut

Draw a picture of yourself meditating.

- **Meditate and do Metta in the meditation hut,** before watching a really funny movie.

- **Mindfully tidy up any mess** left over from the meditation sleepover.

Meditation Campout

- **Invite meditation buddies over and pitch a tent outdoors** (or make one).

- **Before it gets dark, practice silent walking meditation.** When it gets darker out, try doing it with a flashlight, but slowly.

- **Practice listening meditation in your tent after dark.** Sit silently and become aware of any sounds that you hear. Don't like or dislike them, just listen.

= See "Practice walking meditation" on page 71. It's cool to do!

Your Meditation Friends!

Try these...

Mitchell's Meditation Journal

- **Keep a meditation journal.** Write your feelings, thoughts, and experiences down about meditation. How does it make you feel? How does your body feel? What differences do you notice from meditating? Write about change taking place. Draw change you see happening and meditation pictures.

- **Take the Hoffsteader mindfulness challenge.** *IF YOU DARE!* Every morning before you get out of bed, see if you can notice one breath going in and out! Then get up.

- **Wash your hands, sit quietly, and observe them air-drying.** This is fun to do with other meditators.

- **Practice walking meditation.** Here's how! Pay attention to your feet as you walk. Notice how they feel. Be mindful of your entire body as you walk. Try walking with shoes on and off.

  Try walking on different surfaces, like carpet or grass. Walk at different paces mindfully. *Try backwards walking mindfully.* Notice your breath as you walk. Be mindful of your overall walking experience.

- **Choose a food that you really don't like much, but one you're not totally grossed out by and that you're willing to eat.** (For me it's definitely peas! Double yuck!!) In silence, really look at the food, smell it, and then slowly chew and eat the food. Really taste it. Do this mindfully without judging it. Do you feel the same way toward the food?

- **Practice brushing your teeth mindfully** using your flashlight awareness.

Decoder Page

by Mitchell H.

Liam

Definitions from the Hoffsteader Book of Knowledge.

Mindful — A cool way to be. It's when your mind is calm, balanced, and in the present moment. You're aware of what you are doing. It's when you have flashlight awareness shining on whatever you're doing and experiencing. You are not grossed out and complaining about it or loving it so much you have to marry it. It's peacefully paying attention, on purpose, in the moment.

Foundling — The opposite of lostling. Someone who's been dropped off somewhere unknown to them. They are then found by someone else who declares, "Oh, look, a foundling!"

Persnickety — A personality condition worse and more feared than uppity.

DNA — Twines of codes for what I am and what I look like. Determines <u>N</u>aturally <u>A</u>ll-we-are. Betzilla claims it has to do with Deoxyribonucleic Acid ...ah, my omniscient plucky gray matter molecules continue to decipher her perplexing data!

Tibet — A beautiful and very noble country where Tibetans and Yaks live. Birthplace of our friend, His Holiness the Dalai Lama.

Betzilla — Almost human-like creature with glasses. Runs at top speed. Can jump piles of toys when chasing its prey. Beware!

This must be Mitchell's Decoder Page!

Buddha

Gautama Buddha was a cool guy who lived a long time ago in India. First he was a real rich prince. He gave that all up to learn the truth about himself and life. He discovered how he and others could be free from all humanoid suffering.

"Why is G. Buddha cool?" you may ask. 'Cause he taught anyone who wanted to know how to be truly happy and peaceful instead of unhappy and miserable.

He got them to realize they caused their own unhappiness. This was because of attachment and self-centered thinking. I I I, me me me, mine mine mine thinking.

He helped people understand that all things are impermanent. Even us. So every moment is precious.

Best of all, he taught kids and adults how to meditate so they could become happy and peaceful. ☺

G. Buddha was called "the awakened one" because his mind was peaceful and only full of love and compassion.

Mr. Buddha knew that everyone and everything in the universe was interconnected. So it is important to be kind to everyone everywhere.

P.S. I wish I could take Gautama to "show and tell" day at school. He could teach everyone how to meditate. Then I could take him skateboarding with me.   G. Buddha is awesome!

Remember, the Universe is inside you

Be Happy